JESUS
LIGHTS THE SABBATH LAMP

A story of what might have happened one day when Jesus was a child.

JAMES S. TIPPETT

Illustrated by Nell Fisher

ISBN 0-687-09025-3

ABINGDON PRESS
MANUFACTURED IN HONG KONG

99 00 01 02 03 04 05 06 07 08 – 10 9 8 7 6 5 4 3 2 1

The day was hot.

Jesus liked eating under the old olive tree.

His mother, Mary, was holding baby Joses on her lap.

His brother, James, stood beside their father, Joseph.

Jesus looked at the steps going up outside the low house.

Doves cooed on the low wall around the roof.

The sun was going down.

"The roof will be pleasant for sleeping tonight," Mary said.

"I will help spread the mats for our beds," Jesus said.

Jesus went up the steps with his mother.

He helped her spread mats on the flat roof.

"Look, Mother!" he said. "The sun has gone down."

"Tomorrow at sundown our Sabbath will begin," Mary said. "Then the Sabbath lamp will be lighted."

"Mother," Jesus said, "I want to do something special for this Sabbath."

"There will be much to do," his mother said. "You may help. But first we must all sleep."

Jesus and his mother went down the steps.

"You may take James to his mat now," Mary told Jesus.

Jesus led James by the hand up the steps to his mat.

"Big mats for Father and Mother. Little mats for baby Joses and you. An in-between mat for me," Jesus said.

Soon the others were asleep.

Jesus looked at the shining stars.

"The heavens declare the glory of God," he said softly. "I want to do something special for God."

Jesus awakened early.

"May I go with you to the carpenter shop?" he asked Joseph.

"We will go soon," Joseph answered.

As they left the house, Jesus stood on tiptoe to touch a little box on the doorpost.

Words inside it said:

LOVE GOD WITH ALL YOUR HEART.

Jesus kissed his fingers.

They had touched the mezuzah.

In the carpenter shop Jesus helped bring out the tools. He picked up pieces of wood.

"Someday I will be big like you," he said to Joseph. "I will be a carpenter and I will help you."

"You help me now," Joseph said.

Jesus kissed his father and ran to help his mother.

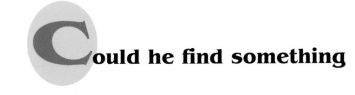

Could he find something special to do?

He played with baby Joses.

He fed the little donkey.

He showed a sparrow's nest to James.

He went to the market with his mother.

They bought fresh oil for the Sabbath lamp.

At last the sun was going down. The Sabbath would soon begin. The Sabbath lamp would be lighted.

"Mother," Jesus said, "I wanted to do something special to show my love for God."

"You have been helpful all day," Mary answered. "That is one way to show your love for God."

Joseph came home from work. He bathed and dressed himself go to the synagogue.

As he left the small house, Joseph touched the mezuzah on the doorpost. He kissed his fingers.

"Love God with all your heart," he said.

"It is time now for the Sabbath lamp to be lighted," Mary said.

Jesus watched his mother. She always lighted the Sabbath lamp. Jesus waited for her to do it now.

"My son," Mary said to Jesus, "you have helped us today. Your father and I are well pleased with you. You may light the Sabbath lamp."

Jesus looked at his mother.

His eyes were shining.

"We give thanks to you, O God. We give thanks," he said.

Jesus had been helpful.

He had lighted the Sabbath lamp.

He had said the Sabbath prayer.

He had done something special

to show his love for God.